Beginning Blues Guitar

A Guide to the Essential Chords, Licks, Techniques & Concepts

by Dave Rubin

Check out these other great Hal Leonard books by Dave Rubin:

Boogie Blues Riffs (HL00699621)

12-Bar Blues Riffs (HL00699622)

12-Bar Blues Solos (HL00699765)

Solo Blues Guitar (HL00699719)

Inside the Blues Series:

Art of the Shuffle (HL00695005)

Blues Turnarounds (HL00695602)

Inside the Blues 1942-1982 Updated Edition (HL00695952)

Power Trio Blues (HL00695028)

Rockin' the Blues (HL00695491)

12-Bar Blues (HL00695187)

PLAYBACK+

Speed • Pitch • Balance • Loop

To access audio visit:
www.halleonard.com/mylibrary

7931-3571-7795-3919

ISBN 978-1-4234-0457-6

HAL•LEONARD®

7777 W. BLUEMOUND RD. P.O. BOX 13819 MILWAUKEE, WI 53213

In Australia Contact:
Hal Leonard Australia Pty. Ltd.
4 Lentara Court
Cheltenham, Victoria, 3192 Australia
Email: ausadmin@halleonard.com.au

Visit Hal Leonard Online at
www.halleonard.com

Contents

Introduction

Beginning Blues Guitar could also be simply titled *Beginning Guitar* because the blues is not only the first truly American musical form (along with jazz, which comes from the blues), but the source of virtually all popular music that follows. Therefore, this book could be seen as two-in-one: A guide through the required fundamentals of blues guitar, as well as an introduction to general guitar techniques. All of the most basic—yet important—tools are here: from scales and chords to double stops and string bending. Clear and logical guidance to building solos and becoming an accomplished rhythm guitarist is provided, as is audio for all musical figures. The chordal examples have the added value of functioning as backing tracks; use them to practice the licks, riffs, and solos found in the following pages.

Most of all, this book is meant to be fun. Learning should be fun, especially when it involves the guitar and blues music! To paraphrase Mr. Spock: "Live long and practice."

Dave Rubin
New York City, 2005

Chapter 1:
The 12-bar Blues Form

The *12-bar blues* is a unique cycle of three chord changes spread out over 12 bars, or measures. It contains the (almost) mystical property of being able to indefinitely repeat and sustain interest. The roots of the form go all the way back to the British Isles of the fifteenth century, but they did not become the standard foundation of blues songs until the music of Robert Johnson in the mid-1930s.

The three chords are labeled with the Roman numerals I, IV, and V and are terms you will frequently encounter in the blues. They are derived from the major scale, also known as the Ionian mode or the "do-re-mi" scale. **Figure 1** shows the chords from the E and A major scales, two common blues keys.

Fig. 1

Key of E

E	F#m	G#m	A	B	C#m	D#°	E
I	ii	iii	IV	V	vi	vii	I

Key of A

A	Bm	C#m	D	E	F#m	G#°	A
I	ii	iii	IV	V	vi	vii	I

Note that E, A, and B are the I, IV, and V chords in the key of E; and A, D, and E are the I, IV, and V chords in the key of A.

There are two main arrangements of the I, IV, and V chords in a 12-bar blues. The first one is called the "slow change," shown in the key of E in **Figure 2** and heard on **Track 1**. Each chord is strummed four times in each measure.

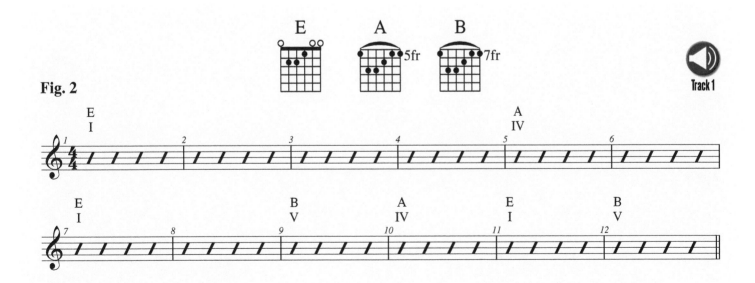

Fig. 2

Figure 3 shows another 12-bar blues progression written out in standard notation and tablature, with the "slow change" in the key of G. This example contains basic open major chords. The 4/4 time signature indicates four quarter notes, or strums, per measure.

Fig. 3

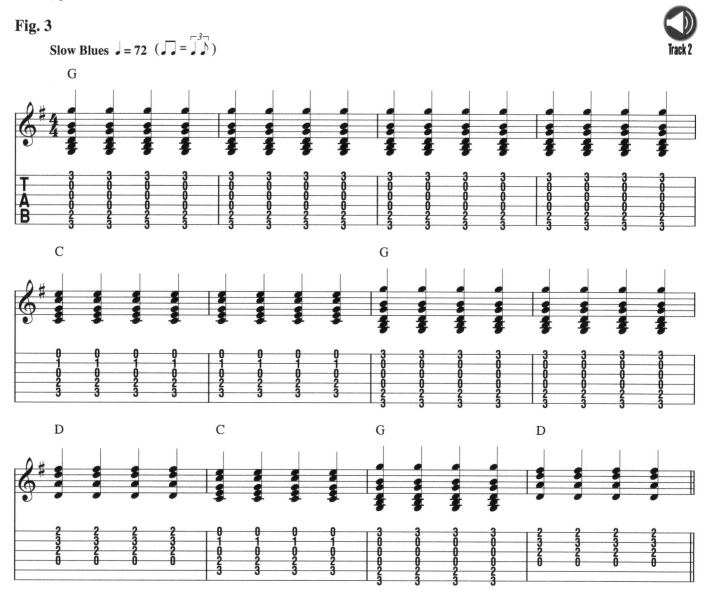

The second arrangement of the 12-bar blues is called the "quick change," shown in **Figure 4** and heard on **Track 3**. Be aware that the only difference between the slow and quick changes occurs in measure 2.

Fig. 4

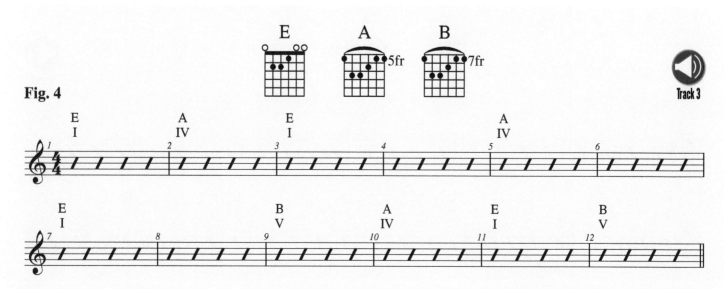

Try this 12-bar blues written out with the "quick change" in the key of C.

Fig. 5

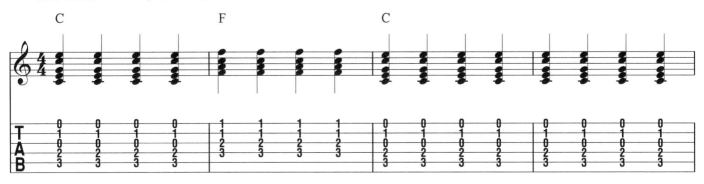

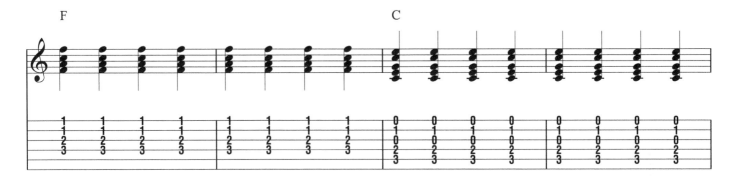

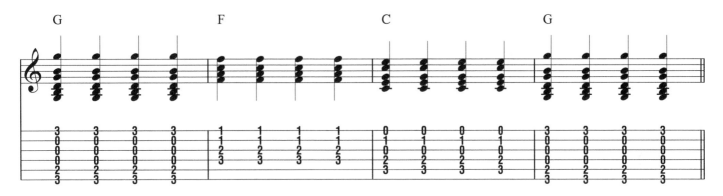

Shuffle Feel

You may have already noticed the distinct rhythm feel of the blues. It is characterized by uneven eighth-note rhythms, called the *shuffle* or *swing feel*, and indicated at the start of the music with this symbol:( ). Basically, eighth notes are played in a "long-short" sequence, where the first eighth note is played twice as long as the second eighth note. This concept is probably best understood by listening and feeling. You'll hear the shuffle feel used on most of the examples in this book. It's a key element of the blues and jazz.

BLUES NUGGET

Though the term "blues," as it relates to depression or melancholia, had been around since the Elizabethan era and "blue devils" referred to boredom circa the early 1800s, author Washington Irving is credited with first using the term "the blues" in 1807 to describe a mood.

While open-string folk-type chords are used extensively in acoustic country blues, more modern blues forms tend to contain barre-chord voicings. Notice that these chords are 7th chords instead of major chords, a crucial characteristic of the blues. This figure also uses a *straight-eighth feel* instead of the shuffle feel from the previous figures. Feel the pulse of the bass line as you strum the quarter-note rhythms.

Fig. 6

Moderate Blues ♩ = 104

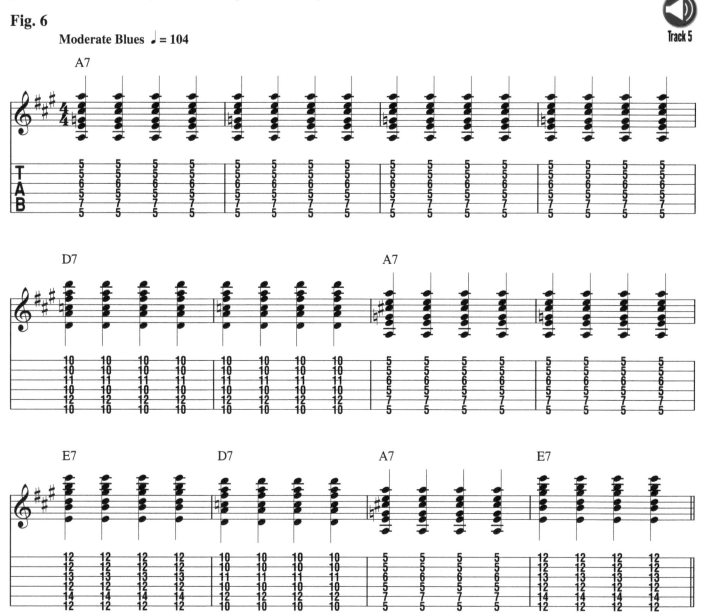

Here's another "quick change" blues with barre chords, shown in **Figure 7** and heard on **Track 6**. This time the rhythm is written in swung eighth notes instead of quarter notes. Also notice a second type of barre chord form for the D7 and E7 chords.

Fig. 7

Slow Blues ♩ = 72

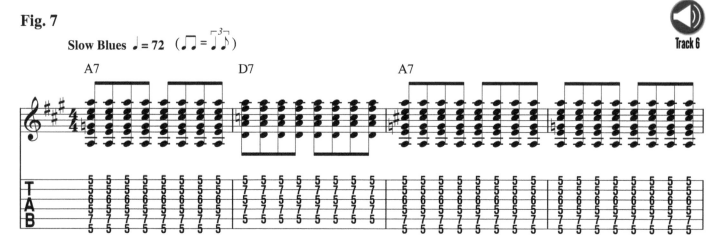

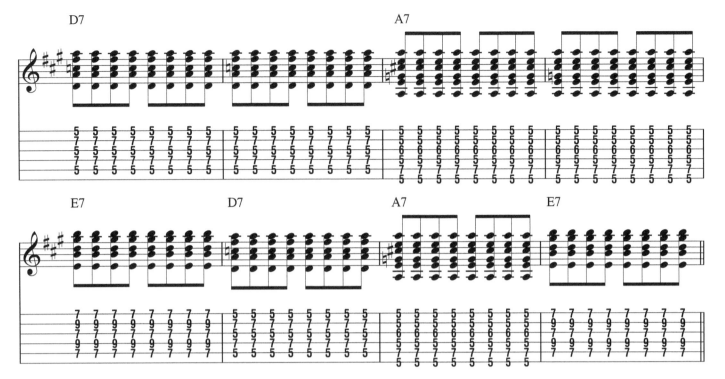

Another common key is the key of D. This last figure is an up-tempo blues with a straight-eighth feel.

Fig. 8

Moderate Blues ♩ = 116

Track 7

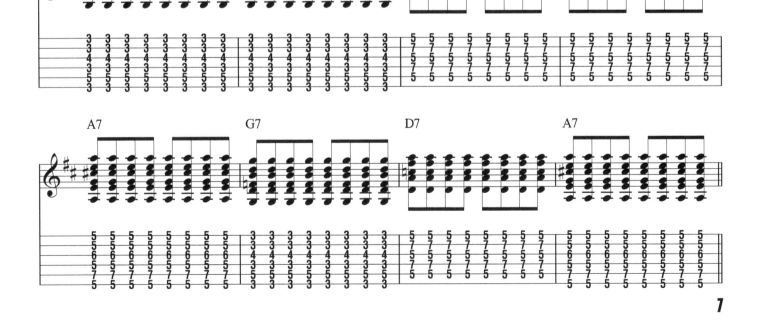

Chapter 2:
Boogie Rhythms

Though mainly associated with the piano, southern guitar players began adapting boogie-woogie to their instruments in the late 1800s. In 1935, Johnny Temple became the first to record "cut boogie" patterns on the guitar, with "Lead Pencil Blues." Later, Robert Johnson would popularize the style with "Sweet Home Chicago" and "Ramblin' On My Mind."

12-bar, Open-string Boogie Patterns in A

A is the only key in which you don't have to use a movable-chord boogie form (see Fig. 13), as all three chord changes may employ open strings. The "cut boogie" pattern, which utilizes 5th and 6th intervals and omits the ♭7th, is the most basic **[Figure 9]**. It's also a very common blues rhythm and a great way to get acquainted with the 12-bar blues form. Keep your first finger planted on the second fret and use your third finger for the fourth fret changes for each chord.

Figure 10 uses a bass-string embellishment and sounds more like the patterns piano players would use. Again, keep your first finger planted on the second fret and use your second and third fingers for the other notes.

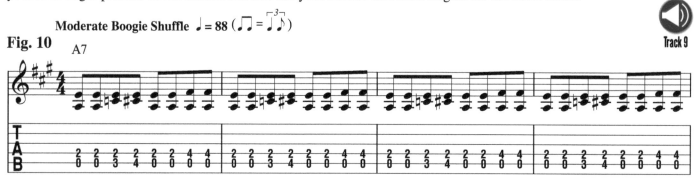

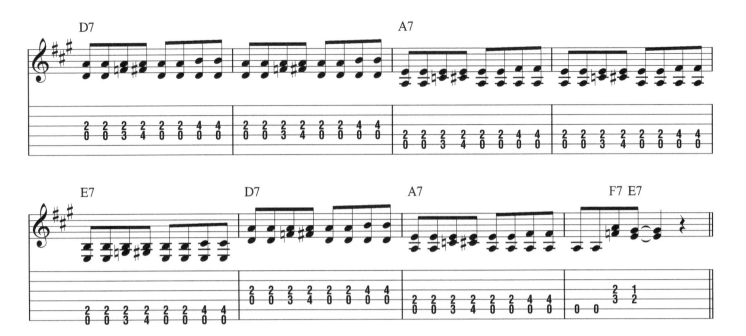

Figure 11 contains 5ths, 6ths *and* ♭7ths, along with the classic boogie bass-string embellishment. Here you'll need to use your pinky finger to play the ♭7th on the fifth fret. Be sure to keep your fingers arched when you play the bass embellishments so all the notes ring out. Beaucoup blues!

Fig. 11

Moderate Boogie Shuffle ♩ = 88 (♫ = ♪♪³)

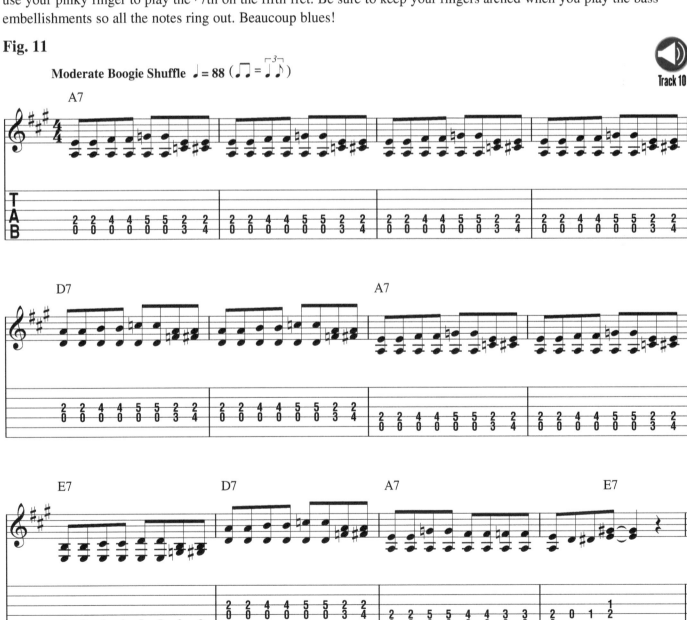

In **Figure 12**, the I (E7) and IV (A7) chord changes employ open-string patterns, as previously shown. However, the V (B7) chord necessitates the use of a movable-chord form. Though a stretch, possessing movable-chord boogie technique is a most worthy goal! Hold down the movable shape with your first and third fingers while rocking your pinky up to play the G♯ on fret 6.

Fig. 12

Moderate Boogie Shuffle ♩ = 88

Track 11

Movable-chord Boogie Patterns

Acquiring the skill to play movable-chord boogie patterns will open up the whole blues world to you. Additionally, the increased strength, agility, and finger independence gained will improve your overall guitar technique. The basic 12-bar pattern in the key of A in **Figure 13** can be transposed to virtually any other key by moving it up and down the fingerboard.

Fig. 13

Moderate Boogie Shuffle ♩ = 84

Track 12

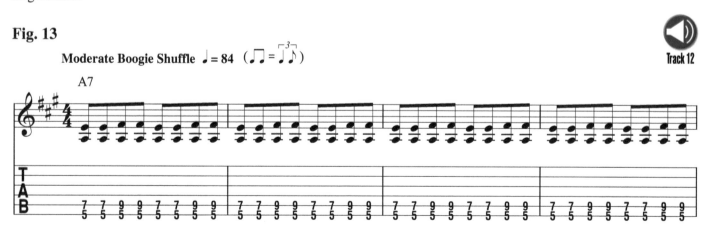

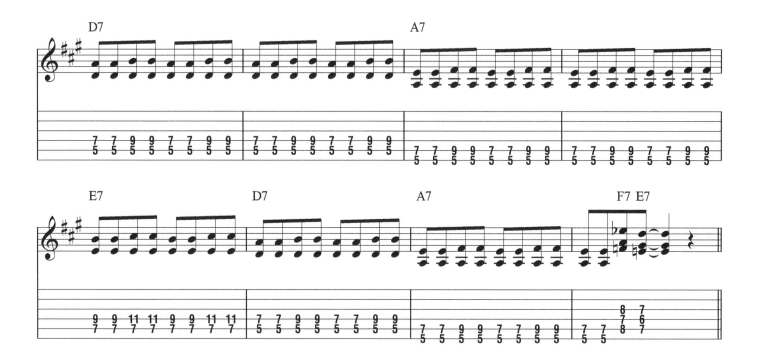

Figure 14 contains the classic blues embellishment used earlier in which the bass line moves from the minor 3rd to the major 3rd on beat 4 of each measure, but this time it's used with the movable-chord forms. Use your pinky to access these notes. Boogie-woogie music is founded upon this concept.

Fig. 14

Moderate Boogie Shuffle ♩ = 84 (♪♪ = ⌐3⌐ ♩♪)

Track 13

Figure 15 utilizes exactly the same pitches as the previous figure. However, instead of moving the IV and V chord changes to the next string pair, all of the patterns occur on strings 5 and 6 for a smoother transition. Both approaches are valid and are mainly a matter of subjective opinion.

Fig. 15

Track 14

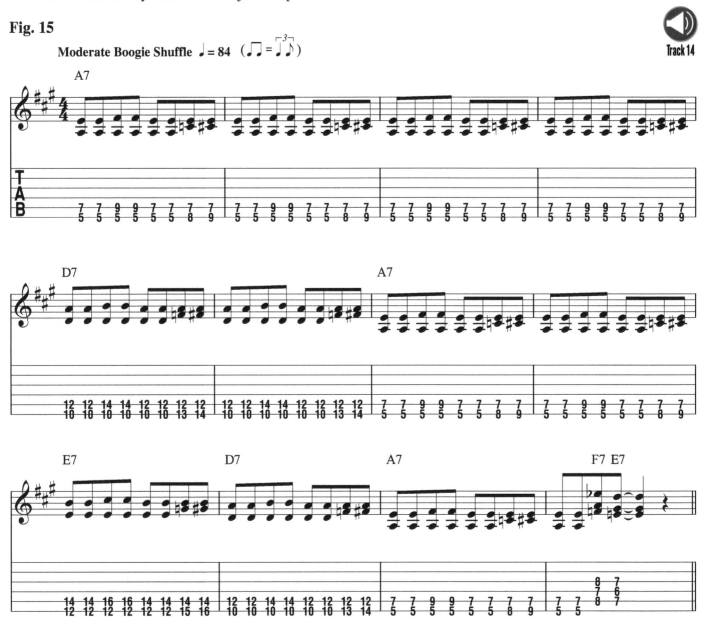

BLUES NUGGET

Hersal Thomas, one of the pioneers of boogie-woogie piano, made his debut in 1924 at the age of 14 and was the brother of the great blues singer Sippie Wallace.

Chapter 3:
The Minor Pentatonic Scale

The vast majority of blues solos and riffs are plucked from the *minor pentatonic scale*. "Pentatonic" means "five tones" and, coincidentally, there are five positions, or *boxes*, of the scale in every key. With its roots stretching back to North Africa and the Middle East, the minor pentatonic scale is the basis of the *blues scale* (see Chapter 4) and beginning blues improvisation. The minor pentatonic scale uses the root, ♭3rd, 4th, 5th, and ♭7th notes (A, C, D, E, and G in the key of A) of the minor scale, which Southern blacks sang as "field hollers" on plantations after the Civil War. Be hip to the fact that though called the *minor* pentatonic scale, it is used in both minor- and major-key blues and rock. This versatility is one of its signature characteristics.

Figure 16 shows the five boxes, or scale positions, of the A minor pentatonic scale. It is imperative that they be committed to memory and then transposed to all other keys. Over time you should assimilate where the root notes occur. You should also know that each box contains the same five notes, but in a different pattern. Notice that the fifth box would join onto the root box, displaced one octave higher, if you continued up the fingerboard. Therefore, the fifth box could be dropped down an octave, to fret 2, as well, joining onto the root box at fret 5.

Besides looking cool (not to be overlooked!), learning to move fluidly between all positions will add welcome variety to your solos.

Fig. 16

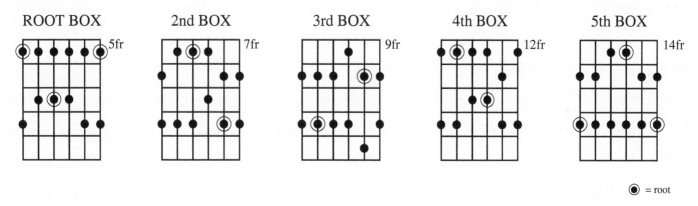

ROOT BOX   2nd BOX   3rd BOX   4th BOX   5th BOX

◉ = root

It's time to combine the "ABCs" (notes) of the minor pentatonic scale into "words" (licks) that will allow you to "speak" (improvise) in complete sentences (solos). Try them at various tempos and don't be afraid to put your own stamp on them in terms of phrasing and feel.

Fig. 17A   **Fig. 17B**   Track 15

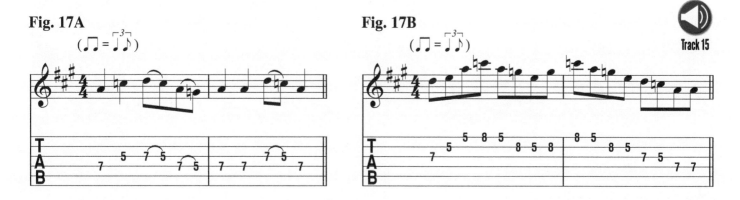

Here is a slow blues solo for you to learn using all five positions of the A minor pentatonic scale. Again, do not be afraid to interpret it using your own personal musical expression. The chord changes in measures 11, 12, 23, and 24 are a classic blues *turnaround*. You'll learn more about turnarounds in Chapter 10.

Fig. 18

Chapter 4:
The Blues Scale

The classic blues scale contains the same five notes as the minor pentatonic scale plus one additional note, the ♭5th (E♭ in the key of A). Its purpose will be further demonstrated in Chapter 8. But for now, practice the five patterns in **Figure 19**, which correspond to the minor pentatonic boxes in **Figure 16**, and get acclimated to the blues scale sound.

Fig. 19

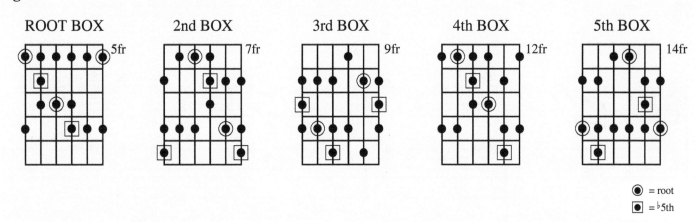

Following are examples of typical licks in each of the five positions of the blues scale. Observe how the ♭5th adds another, darker color to what is essentially the minor pentatonic scale.

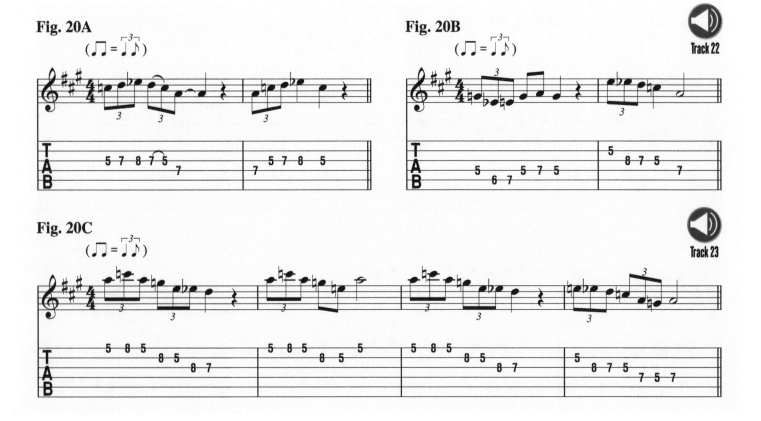

The great Memphis Minnie once bested the great Big Bill Broonzy in a "cutting contest," after which he is reported to have exclaimed, "She plays guitar like a man!"

Take a shot at a 24-measure slow blues solo that employs the blues scale in all five positions, with the ♭5th liberally featured throughout.

Fig. 21

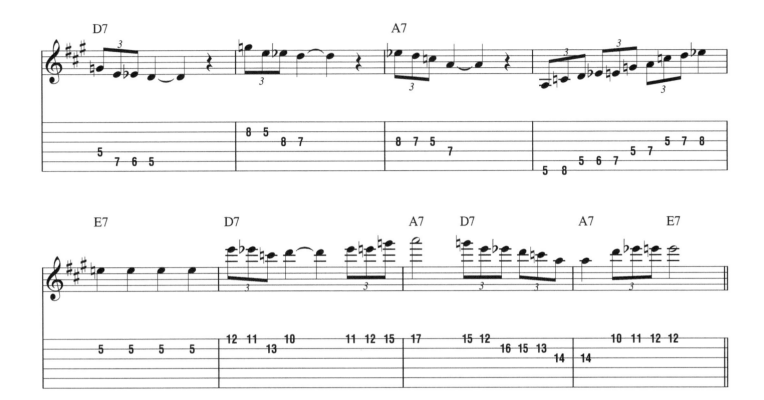

BLUES NUGGET

Blind Willie Johnson was perhaps the greatest slide guitarist of all, equally adept at blues or gospel. Legend has it that he caused a riot when he sang "If I Had My Way I'd Tear the Building Down" in front of the customs house in New Orleans.

Chapter 5:
Chord Accompaniment

Before there were boogie patterns, strummed chords were the accompaniment of choice for recorded blues and still are a major component of the sound. Although they're the most basic chord forms, open chords are still an integral part of country, or "down home," blues. We'll start with open-position chords and progress to barre chords.

12-bar Slow Blues in A with Open Chords

Notice how all three chords are voiced as 7th chords in **Figure 22**, a defining characteristic of the blues. The chords you played in Chapter 1 were also 7th chords, but here open-position 7th chords are featured.

Fig. 22

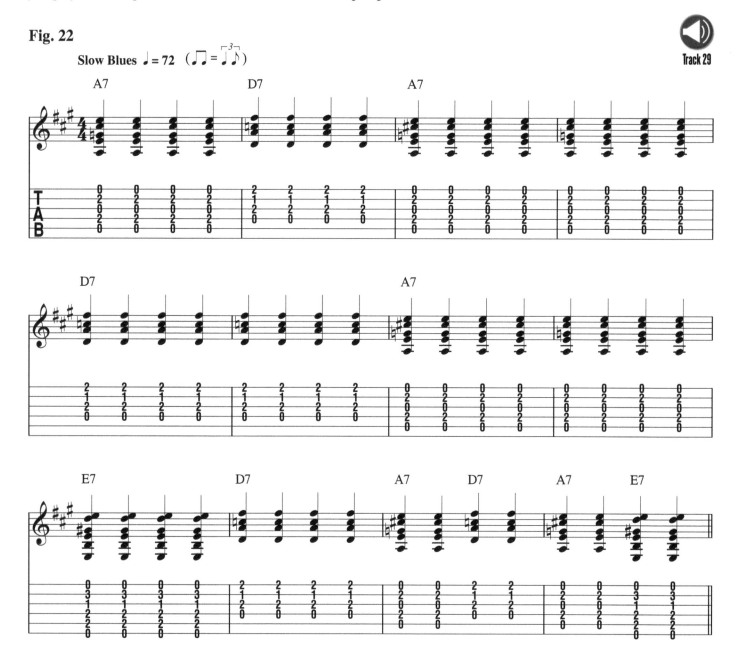

12-bar Slow Blues in E with Open Chords

Figure 23 employs a different voicing of the A7 chord than Fig. 22 in order to blend more smoothly with the B7 chord.

Fig. 23

Track 30

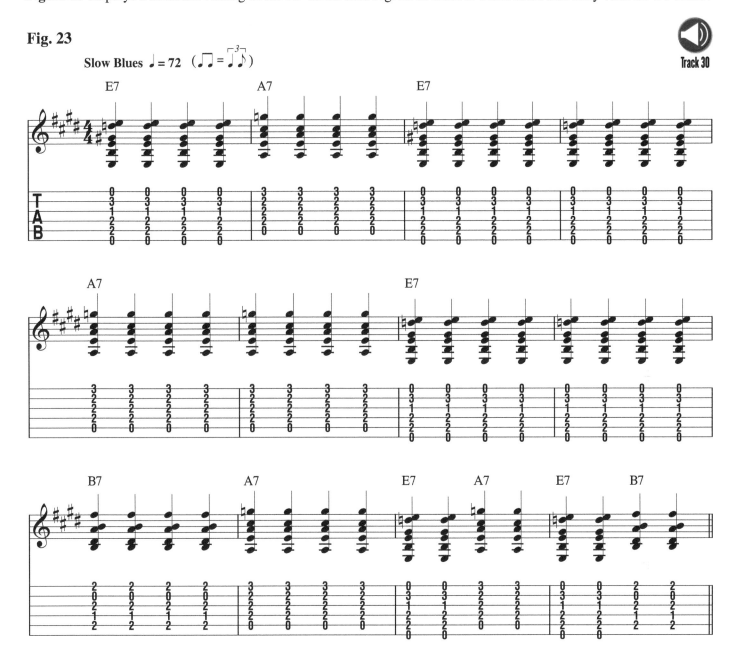

BLUES NUGGET

Charley Patton sometimes went by the pseudonym "Masked Marvel."

12-bar Slow Blues in A with Barre Chords

A new—and important—blues rhythm is introduced in **Figure 24**. Known as 12/8 time, it involves strumming three times (triplets) for each of the four beats of each measure. Also dig the two types of A7 chords utilized to give a heightened sense of forward motion to the progression. Playing barre chords like these for extended periods of time takes real hand and wrist strength, so go slowly with this example. It will be worth the effort, as barre chords allow you to play in all twelve keys.

Fig. 24

Slow Blues ♩. = 72

Track 31

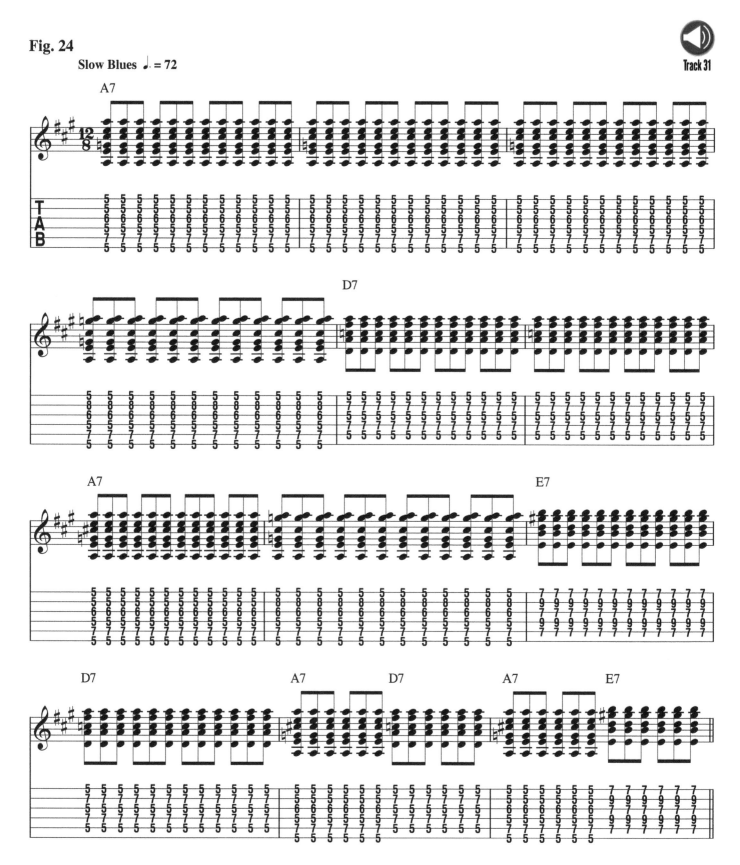

12-bar Slow Blues in E with Barre Chords

Figure 25 shows two common forms of the I (E7), IV (A7), and V (B7) chords. There are others, but these two will get you well on your way to becoming a barre-chord specialist like the late Johnny Ramone. Well, no… not quite. But eventually you'll be able to accompany with authority!

Fig. 25

Slow Blues ♩ = 72

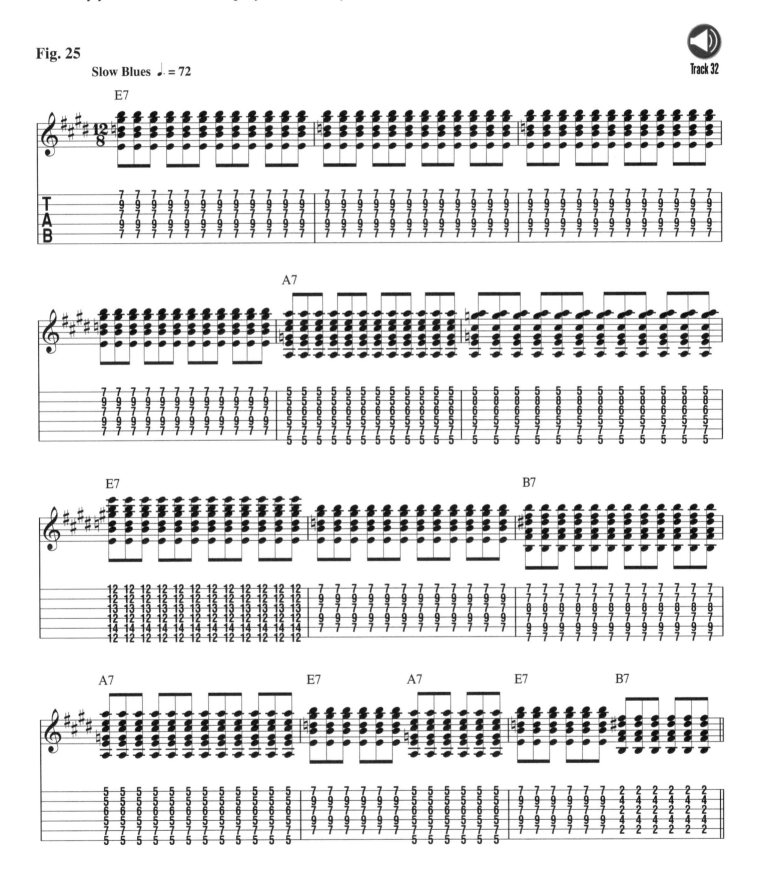

12-bar Swinging Shuffle with Barre Chords

The rhythm in **Figure 26** is colloquially known as the "Charleston Rhythm." It's a classy—and important—technique for playing swinging shuffles favored by Texas guitarists such as T-Bone Walker and Stevie Ray Vaughan.

Fig. 26

8-bar Blues

The interesting thing about *8-bar blues* is that the chords tend to change faster than in 12-bar blues, thus often making them more interesting to play. **Figure 27** is similar to "Key to the Highway," a classic 8-bar blues.

Fig. 27

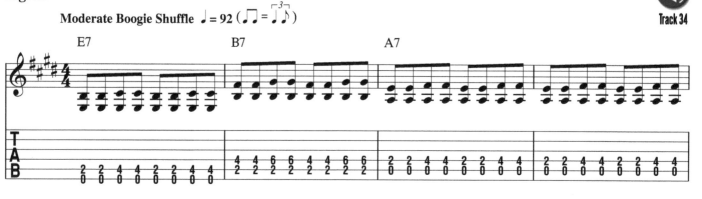

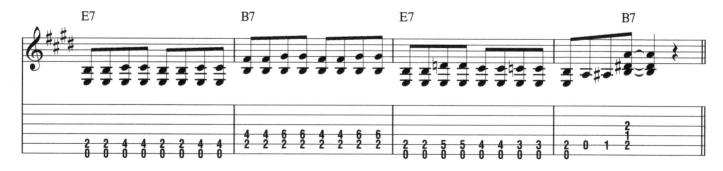

Chapter 6:
The Major Pentatonic Scale

The major pentatonic scale also has five notes, but they differ significantly from the minor pentatonic scale in that they contain the root, 2nd, 3rd, 5th, and 6th degrees of the major scale (A, B, C♯, E, and F♯ in the key of A) for a distinctly major sound. The good news is that it uses exactly the same five boxes as the minor pentatonic scale (Fig. 16), although in a different location on the neck. A simple method for finding the root box of the major pentatonic scale is to move down the neck three frets from the root box of the minor pentatonic or blues scale. For example: If the key of your song is in A, with the root box at fret 5, relocate to fret 2 (which is also F♯ minor pentatonic), as in **Figure 28**.

The major pentatonic scale is a tremendous improvising tool pioneered by B.B. King and picked up by countless other guitarists like Eric Clapton and Stevie Ray Vaughan.

Fig. 28

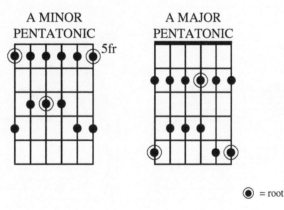

⊚ = root

Get ready to learn and play the sweet side of the blues with hip licks from the major pentatonic scale in five positions.

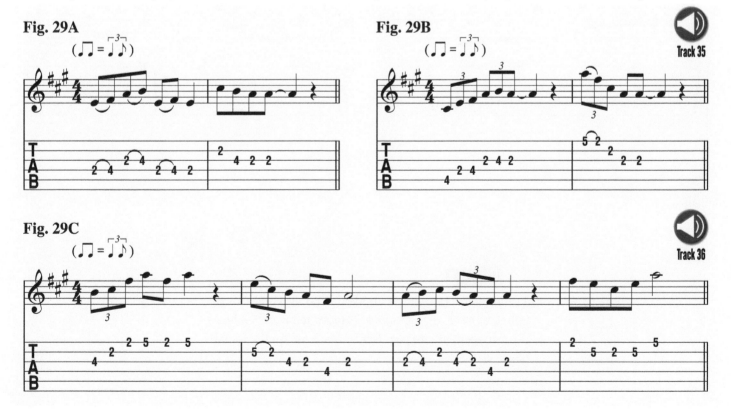

The immortal Howlin' Wolf liked Elvis as a blues singer, telling writer Peter Guralnick: "He started from the blues. If he stopped, he stopped. But he made his 'pull' from the blues."

Play it pretty! Check out the following 24 bars of melodic major pentatonic blues soloing for your edification.

Fig. 30

Chapter 7: String Bending

String bending is to blues guitar what flying is to birds: It's a natural part of the development and is definitely required. Derived from African-American musical tradition and originally employed as a way for guitarists to mimic the swooping "bent notes" sung by vocalists, it is the most expressive and personal component of blues techniques.

Getting a Grip

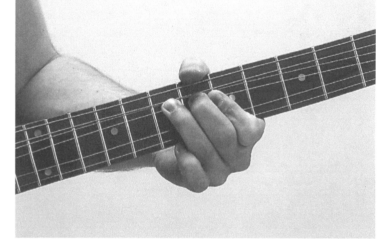

1. Always wrap your thumb over the edge of the fingerboard, near the low E string, in order to squeeze the neck for utmost power when bending. Traditional blues cats called this "choking" the strings, for obvious reasons.
2. When bending with the pinky, ring, or middle finger, reinforce the bending finger with the ring, middle and index; middle and index; or index fingers, respectively, for maximum control and strength (see photo).
3. Adjust the angle of your fingers so that the string makes contact with your fingertip, just below the fingernail.
4. Maintain steady pressure throughout the bend, especially at the peak. Blues-bender extraordinaire Michael Bloomfield claimed it was the secret to long sustain.

BLUES NUGGET

When future blues guitar star Buddy Guy went to Chicago in 1957 to find Muddy Waters, the "Hoochie Coochie Man" gave him a sandwich, a slap in the face, and told him to go and play.

Testing Your Mettle

Let's dig right in and start acquiring chops via the two most common bends in the root position of the minor pentatonic scale. Bend string 3 with your ring finger, reinforced with your middle and index fingers [**Figure 31A**]. Bend string 2 with your pinky, reinforced with your ring, middle, and index fingers [**Figure 31B**].

Track 42

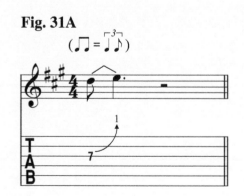

Fig. 31A

Fig. 31B

Classic Blues-scale Bends

Here is a dandy selection of four must-know bending licks in the root position of the A blues scale [**Figures 32A–D**].
Grab 'em while they're hot!

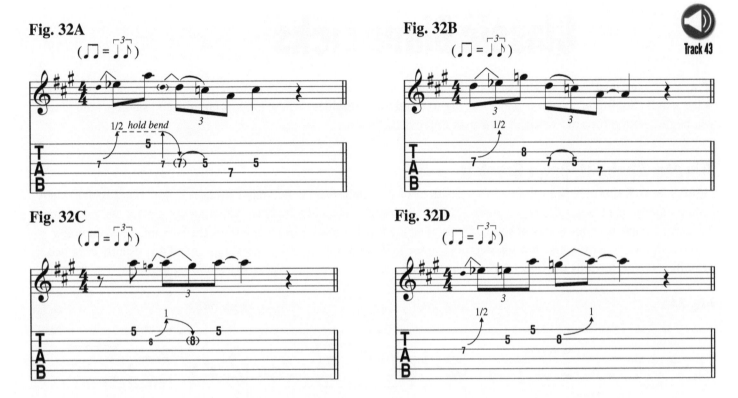

Fig. 32A

Fig. 32B

Track 43

Fig. 32C

Fig. 32D

Bending in the Major Pentatonic Scale

While you *could* execute exactly the same bends in the major pentatonic scale as in the minor pentatonic or blues
scales, the results would not reflect the advantage of its smooth, harmonious sound. Try these four licks [**Figures
33A–D**] on for size from the root position of the A major pentatonic scale (F♯ minor pentatonic).

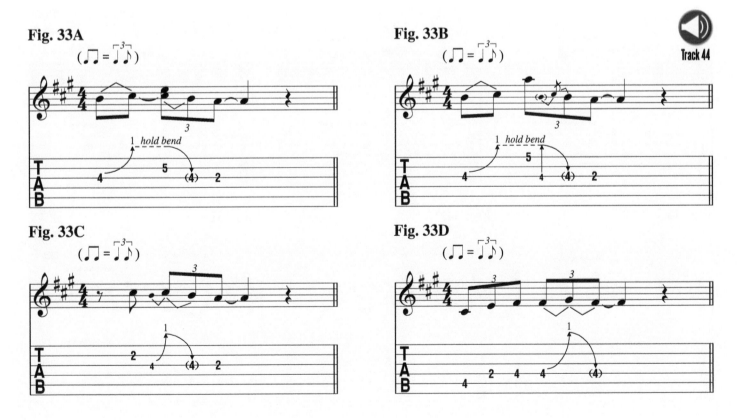

Fig. 33A

Fig. 33B

Track 44

Fig. 33C

Fig. 33D

Chapter 8:
Classic Blues Licks

The blues is a language in which the notes from the scales serve as the letters of the alphabet and the licks function as the words. So, fire up your axe and get ready to acquire a vocabulary of the hippest phrases and sayings around as you begin to build toward "writing" your own improvised "stories."

Vibrato: Shake It, Don't Break It

Figures 34A–X sport hot licks from all five positions of the minor pentatonic, major pentatonic, and blues scales. Many feature *vibrato*, the blues guitarist's signature. Most vibrato is achieved by bending the string up in pitch and returning to the starting pitch at various rates of speed. When combined with a bend, always reinforce the bending-and-vibratoing finger with your other fingers, as suggested in Chapter 7. Vibrato, sans bending, on strings 3 and 4 is usually executed by pulling down (towards the floor) with either the index or ring finger and repeatedly returning to pitch.

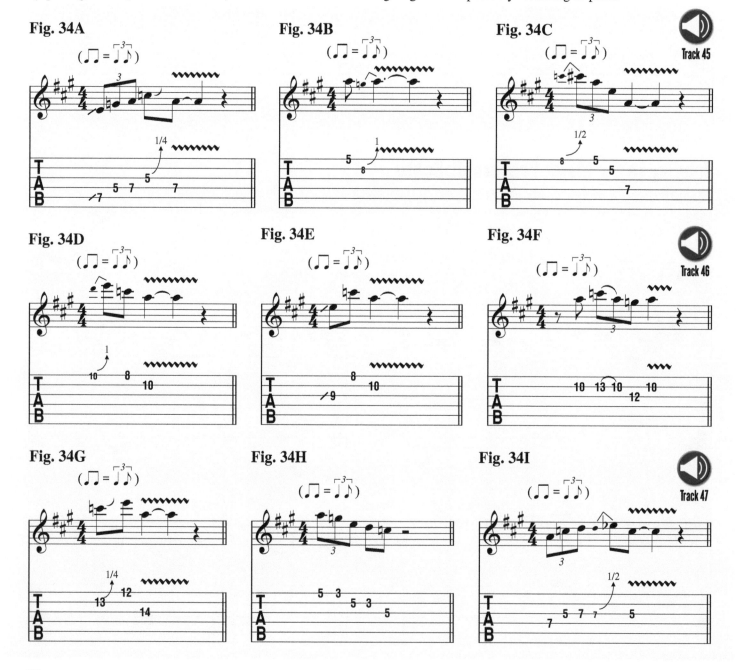

Play the Blues!

Licks and tricks are great, but the secret to playing "real deal" blues is to string them together (pun intended!) to make a coherent musical statement. **Figure 35** is a 12-bar slow blues in the key of A featuring the "quick change" and composed of licks drawn from the blues scale.

Fig. 35

Slow Blues ♩ = 52

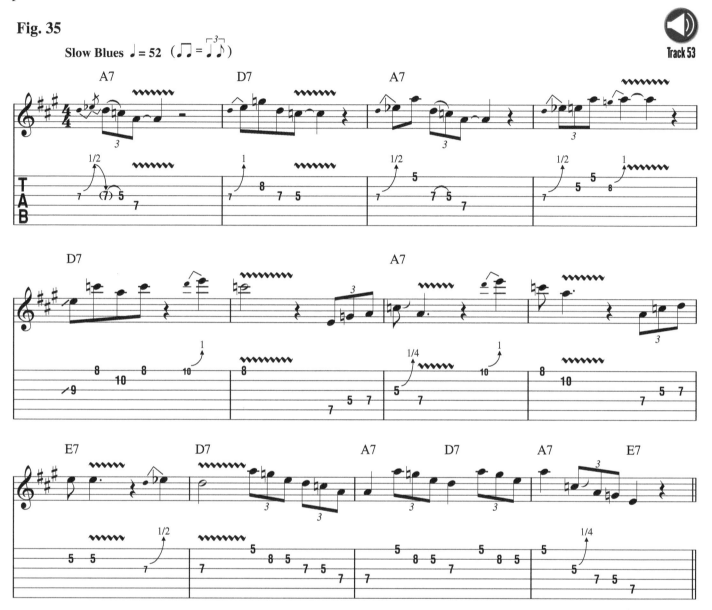

Figure 36 contains a slow blues that features the A major pentatonic (F♯ minor pentatonic) scale. Take note of the sweeter sound when compared to the blues-scale solo in Fig. 35.

Fig. 36

Slow Blues ♩ = 52

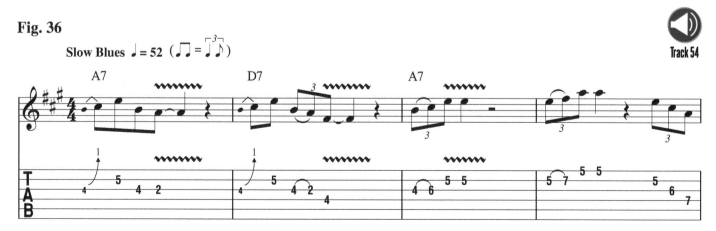

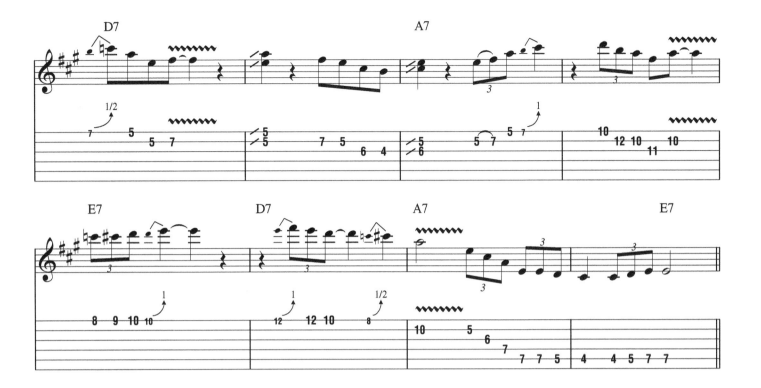

If slow blues (see Chapter 5) are the soul of the genre, then boogie shuffles (see Chapter 2) are the heart of the music. The E minor pentatonic scale is mined for the 12-bar boogie-shuffle solo featuring the "slow change" in **Figure 37**.

Fig. 37

Figure 38 swings the blues via the E major pentatonic (C♯ minor pentatonic) scale. Dig the jazzy vibe.

Fig. 38

Track 56

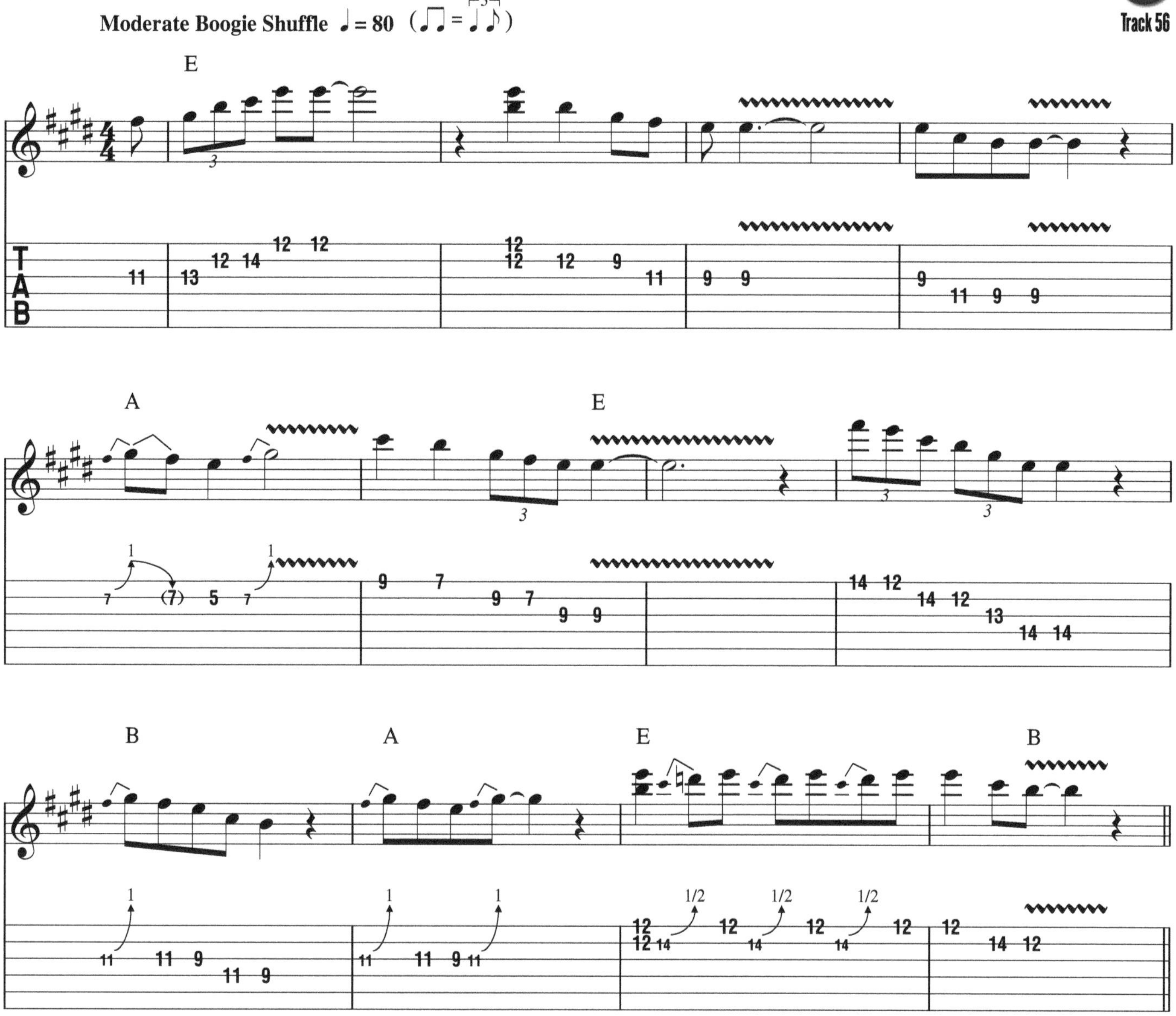
Moderate Boogie Shuffle ♩ = 80
E
A
E
B
A
E
B

BLUES NUGGET

There are more legends about Robert Johnson than any other blues musician. One of the more plausible, given his extraordinary chops, was that he could carry on a conversation with the radio on in the background and the next day accurately play the music that he had heard.

Chapter 9: Double Stops

A chewing-gum company once touted its product with the slogan, "Double your pleasure, double your fun." Now, *double stops* (or *dyads*), the playing of two notes simultaneously, may not literally increase your joy by 100 percent, but they will add significant harmony and substance to your blues playing.

Chuck Berry: Duck-walkin' and Double-stoppin'

In the 1950s, Chuck Berry wrote the book of rock 'n' roll with his use of clanging double stops that were inspired, in part, by guitarists Carl Hogan and Bill Jennings, both of whom played with Louis Jordan a decade earlier. Berry used 3rd- and 4th-interval double stops that can be easily adapted to blues. **Figure 39** shows a combination of 3rd and 4th intervals in the root position of the A blues scale, which was used by Berry to great effect.

Fig. 39

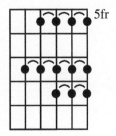

Figures 40A–H are examples of classic blues riffs composed of 3rds in the key of A. Each figure is loosely based on the root and second positions of the A minor pentatonic and/or A major pentatonic scales.

Fig. 40G

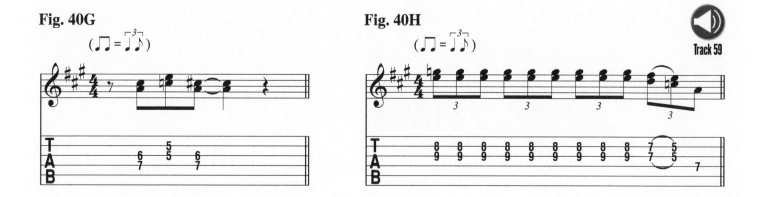

Fig. 40H

Double Your Licks

Though guitarists rarely play entire 12-bar slow-blues solos with double stops, it's a worthy skill to acquire. Notice how the double-stop patterns in **Figure 41**, a solo using 3rd and 4th intervals in the key of A, harmonize the chord change in each measure. However, at this point it's more important to *hear* the connection rather than know the theory behind it.

Fig. 41

Track 60

Like barbecued ribs, moderate and up-tempo instrumental shuffles have spiced the history of blues guitar. Many are composed around double stops similar to those found in **Figure 42**.

Fig. 42

Track 61

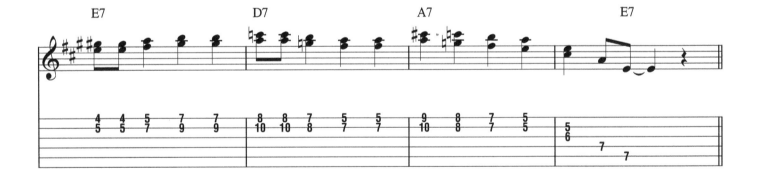

BLUES NUGGET

Huddie "Leadbelly" Ledbetter, the "King of the 12-String Guitar," served several stretches in prison for violent crimes, but once secured a pardon in 1925 by singing for the governor of Texas.

Chapter 10: Intros and Turnarounds

To paraphrase the late Who drummer Keith Moon regarding the art of the solo: "Make a strong entrance and exit, and no one will remember what you played in the middle." Now, "Moonie" was surely no blues cat and may have been underestimating the importance of the body of a solo, but his sentiment could certainly apply to the construction of a blues song.

BLUES NUGGET

Bluesman Robert Shaw was quoted as saying, "When you listen to what I'm playing, you got to see in your mind all them gals out there swinging their butts and gettin' the mens excited. Otherwise, you ain't got the music rightly understood."

Classic Intros

Typically, intros tend to be either two or four measures in length. **Figures 43A–D** "introduce" a selection of the two-measure variety that can be similar to turnarounds, as you will see.

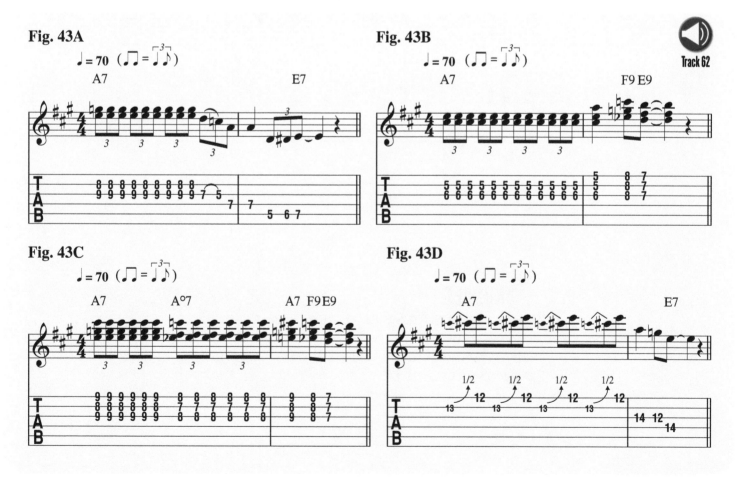

Four-measure intros are less common, but allow for the creation of more anticipation before a blues verse kicks in and are well worth having under your fingers.

Fig. 44A

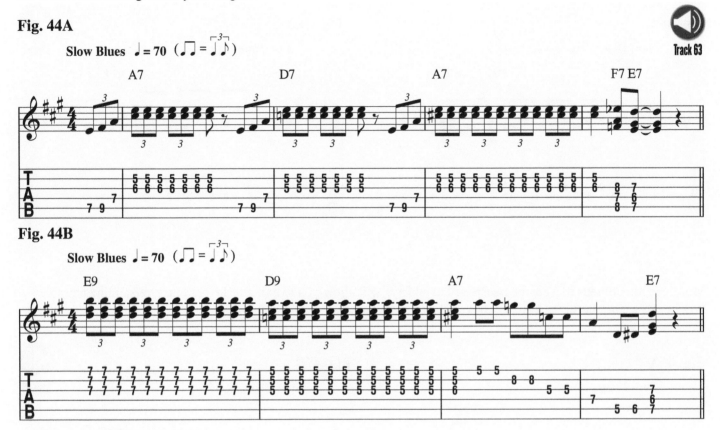

Fig. 44B

Classic Turnarounds

Turnarounds do just that: they turn you back around to the beginning of your blues verse and always appear in measures 11 and 12 of a 12-bar blues. Here is a group of four open-string country-blues turnarounds so down-home you'll think you've time-traveled back, pickin' and grinnin', to the Mississippi Delta.

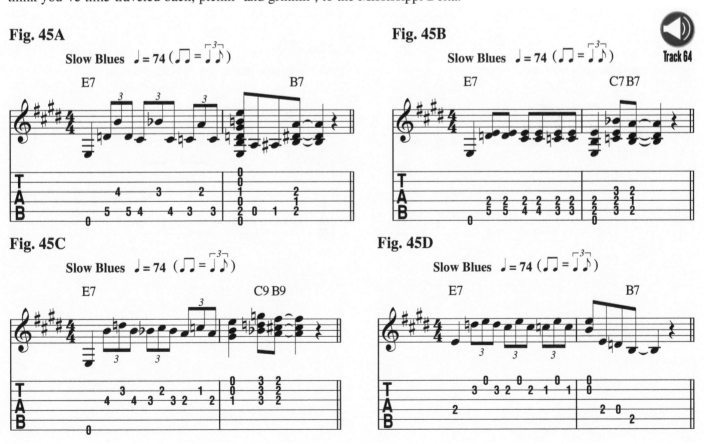

Fig. 45A

Fig. 45B

Fig. 45C

Fig. 45D

These two open-string turnarounds, in the key of A, are quite useful and will help to bolster your blues cred.

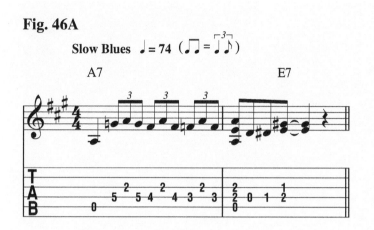

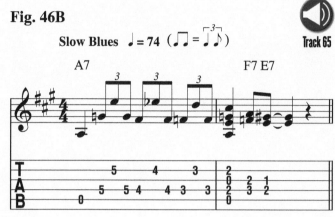

Moveable turnarounds that can be transposed to all keys will allow you to exit any 12-bar blues verse in memorable fashion. Here are four in the key of A that will let people know who you are.

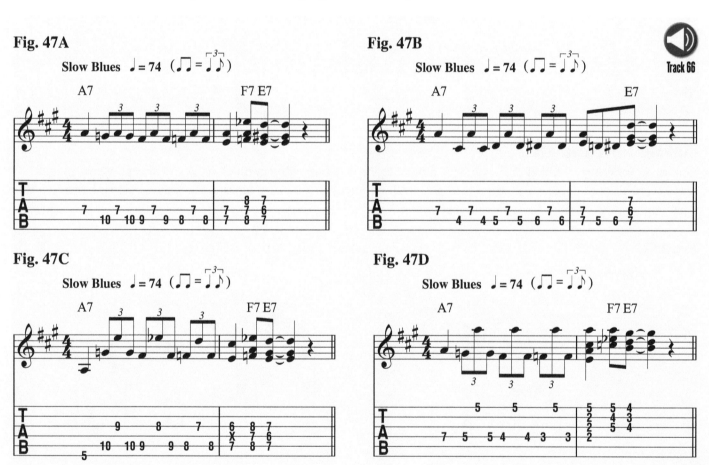

Chapter 11:
Riff Blues

Riffs are some of the most characteristic sounds of the blues. In a nutshell, they may be constructed of bass lines, double stops, or single notes—or a combination thereof. **Figure 48** is a classic example that contains bass lines and double stops which form a catchy, repeatable riff. Notice how the bass line is the same for the I, IV, and V chords, save each chord's respective root note.

Fig. 48

Jazz alto-saxophone legend Charlie "Yardbird" Parker, who was a great blues player, wrote a song called "Thriving on a Riff."

Figure 49 alternates measures of walking bass lines with measures of double stops to create a more expansive riff pattern. Dig how the bass line follows each chord change while the I-chord double stops contain only one different note than the IV-chord double stops.

Fig. 49

Chapter 12:
Creating Blues Solos

If you have prudently studied the previous chapters, you are now ready to apply all of your knowledge to the performance of 12-bar blues solos, including intros, single-note licks, double-stops, and turnarounds. **Figures 50–53** function as a review of the aforementioned material and should also inspire you to begin improvising with personal expression.

Fig. 50

Fig. 51

Moderate Shuffle ♩ = 94

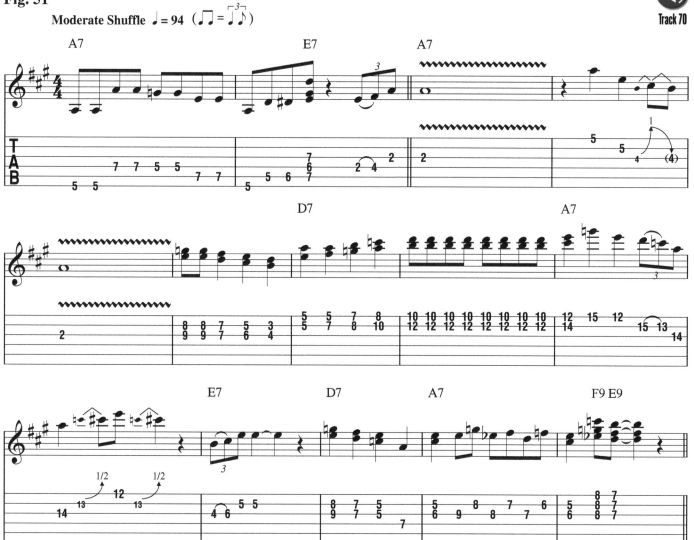

BLUES NUGGET

When Sam Hopkins made recordings with Wilson "Thunder" Smith, the engineer decided to call them "Thunder and Lightnin'," and the nickname stuck with Sam.

Fig. 52

Slow Blues ♩ = 58

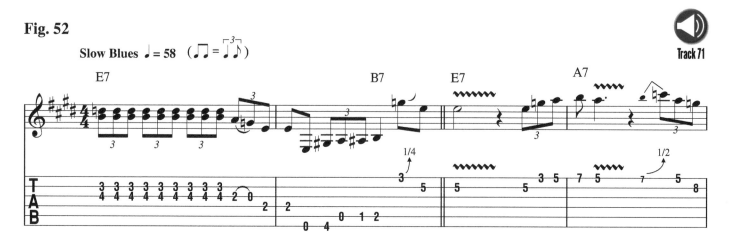

Fig. 53

Moderate Shuffle ♩ = 88

Track 72

Chapter 13: Getting the Sound

If you started with Chapter 1 and worked your way through the book to this point, you should have a good grasp of the most important technical elements of blues guitar. However, another part of the secret to playing great blues is the *sound*. Both T-Bone Walker and jazzman Charlie Christian knew from the dawn of the first commercially-produced electric guitar in 1936 that what they had was not just a *louder* acoustic guitar. When fortuitously combined with primitive tube amps that were incapable of playing "clean," those early electrics produced a fat, raw, sustaining, harmonically rich sound that allowed cats like Walker and Christian and their followers to compete with saxophonists for solo space. By the time Leo Fender & Co. started producing their first great amps, the "tweeds," in the 1950s, the template had been etched for the blues sound. Reverb, arriving in the early 1960s (again courtesy of Fender), was the last significant element in the tonal stew. Essentially, that amp tone—or a similar one—has remained the coveted sound to this day because of its expressive qualities.

Guitars have evolved considerably since Gibson's seminal ES-150, a thin, hollow arch-top. In fact, old-timers often used off-brand axes through cheap tube amps to wail their blues. Use the following classic blues guitar/amp combinations as a guide to find one that works for you.

- **Gibson ES-335/Fender Twin:** The thinline, semi-hollow double-cutaway with humbuckers will sing with warmth, clarity, and sustain through the big Fender combo amp. Check out B.B. King's *Live at the Regal* for a royal taste.

- **Fender Strat/Fender Deluxe Reverb:** The relatively low-output, clean sparkle of the Strat's single-coil pickups will retain its bite while gaining heft when the 20-watt portable Fender is cranked to near-capacity. Stevie Ray Vaughan preferred vintage Vibro Verbs, but you will get the idea on *Texas Flood*.

- **Gibson Les Paul/Marshall Bluesbreakers Combo:** Eric Clapton started a sonic revolution when he matched the harmonically rich sound and massive sustain of a Les Paul Standard sporting PAF humbuckers with a 45-watt Marshall. *Bluesbreakers: John Mayall with Eric Clapton*, with Slowhand's liquid tone and snaky phrasing, still stuns.

- **Gibson ES-125/Fender Princeton:** The thin hollowbody with high-output, single-coil P-90 pickups has a deep, woody tone that emits a surprisingly big and nasty roar when crunched through the little 12-watt Fender. George Thorogood honks on "Who Do You Love" and "Bad to the Bone" with this setup.

- **Fender Strat/Fender Bassman:** For many, this is *the* blues guitar sound. The tweed Bassman (late 1950s vintage or reissue) with 50 watts and four 10-inch speakers needs to be pushed hard, but the result is something like a lower-volume Marshall stack. No wonder—the British tube heavyweight is based on the Fender design. Buddy Guy, among many others, still talks wistfully about the Bassman. Try Son Seals' *Live and Burning* for a dollop of this thrilling tone, even though he was playing a Guild thinline at the time.

Nothing compares in pure visceral blues power to a great tube amp on 10, but this is often impractical, even with smaller varieties. The trick for most electric blues guitarists, then, is getting an acceptable distorted sound at low levels of volume. Beside the master volume control on many modern amps, another effective and efficient way is to use a distortion box. There are countless models to choose from, most of which are completely solid-state or digital, though some actually have built-in tubes. In the end, it becomes a very subjective decision, but the Ibanez Tube Screamer is one of the best and was popularized by Stevie Ray Vaughan. Be aware that there are several models with noticeable differences. Most players prefer the smooth TS-8, as SRV did, but the TS-9 is fairly close and both have been reissued, as the vintage models are prohibitively pricey. Avoid the TS-10 model.

Chapter 14:
Essential Blues Guitar Recordings

Michael Bloomfield *Essential Blues 1964–1969* (Columbia/Legacy CK 57631)

Clarence "Gatemouth" Brown *The Original Peacock Recordings* (Rounder CD 2039)

Roy Buchanan *Second Album* (Polydor 83412)

Albert Collins *Ice Pickin'* (Alligator ALCD 4713)

Guitar Slim *The Things I Used to Do* (Ace CHD 110)

Buddy Guy *Stone Crazy* (Alligator ALCD 4723)

John Lee Hooker *The Very Best of John Lee Hooker* (Rhino 71915)

Howlin' Wolf *The Chess Box* (CHD3-9332)

Lonnie Johnson *Steppin' on the Blues* (Columbia CK 46221)

Robert Johnson *The Complete Recordings* (Columbia C3 46222)

Albert King *Born Under a Bad Sign* (Stax 8606)

B.B. King *King of the Blues* (MCA MCAD4-10677)

Freddie King *Just Pickin'* (Modern Blues 721)

Little Milton *Greatest Hits (Chess 50th Anniversary Collection)* (Chess 9386)

Lonnie Mack *Memphis Wham!* (Ace 713)

Magic Sam *Black Magic* (Delmark 620)

Johnny Moore *Driftin' & Dreamin'* (Ace 589)

Muddy Waters *The Chess Box* (Chess CHD3-80002)

Jimmy Reed *Best of Jimmy Reed* (GNP Crescendo 10006)

Otis Rush *Essential Collection: The Classic Cobra Recordings 1956–1958* (Varese 61077)

Stevie Ray Vaughan *Texas Flood* (Epic 38734)

T-Bone Walker *The Complete Imperial Recordings 1950–1954* (Capitol 96737)

Guitar Notation Legend

Guitar music can be notated three different ways: on a *musical staff*, in *tablature*, and in *rhythm slashes*.

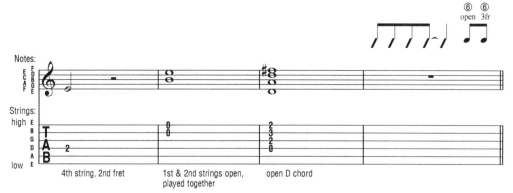

RHYTHM SLASHES are written above the staff. Strum chords in the rhythm indicated. Use the chord diagrams found at the top of the first page of the transcription for the appropriate chord voicings. Round noteheads indicate single notes.

THE MUSICAL STAFF shows pitches and rhythms and is divided by bar lines into measures. Pitches are named after the first seven letters of the alphabet.

TABLATURE graphically represents the guitar fingerboard. Each horizontal line represents a string, and each number represents a fret.

4th string, 2nd fret   1st & 2nd strings open, played together   open D chord

HALF-STEP BEND: Strike the note and bend up 1/2 step.

WHOLE-STEP BEND: Strike the note and bend up one step.

GRACE NOTE BEND: Strike the note and immediately bend up as indicated.

SLIGHT (MICROTONE) BEND: Strike the note and bend up 1/4 step.

BEND AND RELEASE: Strike the note and bend up as indicated, then release back to the original note. Only the first note is struck.

PRE-BEND: Bend the note as indicated, then strike it.

VIBRATO: The string is vibrated by rapidly bending and releasing the note with the fretting hand.

WIDE VIBRATO: The pitch is varied to a greater degree by vibrating with the fretting hand.

HAMMER-ON: Strike the first (lower) note with one finger, then sound the higher note (on the same string) with another finger by fretting it without picking.

PULL-OFF: Place both fingers on the notes to be sounded. Strike the first note and without picking, pull the finger off to sound the second (lower) note.

LEGATO SLIDE: Strike the first note and then slide the same fret-hand finger up or down to the second note. The second note is not struck.

SHIFT SLIDE: Same as legato slide, except the second note is struck.

TRILL: Very rapidly alternate between the notes indicated by continuously hammering on and pulling off.

TAPPING: Hammer ("tap") the fret indicated with the pick-hand index or middle finger and pull off to the note fretted by the fret hand.

NATURAL HARMONIC: Strike the note while the fret-hand lightly touches the string directly over the fret indicated.

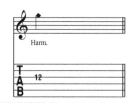

PINCH HARMONIC: The note is fretted normally and a harmonic is produced by adding the edge of the thumb or the tip of the index finger of the pick hand to the normal pick attack.

PICK SCRAPE: The edge of the pick is rubbed down (or up) the string, producing a scratchy sound.

MUFFLED STRINGS: A percussive sound is produced by laying the fret hand across the string(s) without depressing, and striking them with the pick hand.

PALM MUTING: The note is partially muted by the pick hand lightly touching the string(s) just before the bridge.

RAKE: Drag the pick across the strings indicated with a single motion.

TREMOLO PICKING: The note is picked as rapidly and continuously as possible.

VIBRATO BAR DIVE AND RETURN: The pitch of the note or chord is dropped a specified number of steps (in rhythm), then returned to the original pitch.

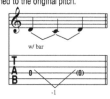

VIBRATO BAR SCOOP: Depress the bar just before striking the note, then quickly release the bar.

VIBRATO BAR DIP: Strike the note and then immediately drop a specified number of steps, then release back to the original pitch.